THE FAITH
OF A WINNER

FAITH PRINCIPLES FOR
THE GROWING CHRISTIAN

*Now the just shall live by faith: but if any man draw
back, my soul shall have no pleasure in him.*

ANTOINE D. JACKSON

The Faith Of A Winner: Principles For The Growing Christian

© 2016 by Antoine D. Jackson

All Scripture quotations, unless otherwise indicated, are taken from the Holy Bible, King James Version, KJV. 1987 Printing. The KJV is public domain in the United States.

ISBN 978-0-692-31523-1

Published by Antoine D. Jackson of Sow Graphics & Publications, LLC

Book Cover and Interior Design by Sow Graphics & Publications, LLC, www.SowGP.com
Editing by Tenita Johnson of So It Is Written, LLC, www.soitiswritten.net

Cover images used under license from Colourbox.com

Printed in the United States of America

Dedication

To my amazing daughter, Madison, you are an inspiration to my life. You are a reminder of God's love and grace commended to me. I remain in awe of your growing personality, skill and intellect. You are daddy's inspiration and motivation.

To believers everywhere, those who aspire to live a life of faith and make a difference in the world.

CONTENTS

Acknowledgments

Many people are deserving of a word of appreciation for helping bring this project to completion.

I remain humbled and thankful to God for allowing me to share what He has given me with the world at large. I am thankful for the joy of the Lord, which is my strength, and the power of the Holy Spirit that lives within me.

To my mentors, my pastor, Bishop John H. Sheard; Mr. Michael Williams; Superintendent Ethan Sheard; and Elder Nic South, I owe you a large debt of gratitude. Each of you, in your own way, has inspired me to continue my journey and pursue excellence in all that I do.

INTRODUCTION

ON ASSIGNMENT

In Hebrews 10:38, our principal text, the writer penned an encouraging letter to the believer. In this the nineteenth book of the twenty-seven in the New Testament, many believe Hebrews 10:38 to have been authored by several writers. However, numerous Bible scholars and students would easily say that the Apostle Paul is mostly responsible for writing this book, arguing that the writing style and voice are closely similar to that of Paul's other writings.

The purpose of the book of Hebrews was to present to the intended audience the sufficiency and superiority of Christ. Although directed primarily at Hebrew Christians, the book is filled with information comparing the old and new covenants in an effort to show how Christ's coming into the earth was a fulfillment of what was only a type and shadow in the Old Testament. The writer of Hebrews presents, over and over again, two major themes: Christ's supremacy and the importance of faith.

The writer wanted us to be certain that Jesus is greater than everyone and everything else. He wanted us to understand that Jesus is greater than the angels, the Old Testament prophets, Moses and David. That importance impelled me to pen this literary work. Romans 10:17 says, *So then faith cometh by hearing, and hearing by the word of God.*

The writer of Hebrews wrote to a people who were tempted to return to their old, outdated customs of religious practices. They wanted to go back to how things used to be. For many of them, they wanted to go backward because of the persecution they were facing. These people were beaten, jailed and scolded for their preaching, teaching and belief in Jesus. So, for many of them, it seemed easier to go back to the former things than to continue on the path toward their unknown future.

Comparably, many today would rather go back to living according to the world's customs, and use outdated methods of survival, instead of trusting in the Lord Jesus Christ. Living for Christ is no walk in the park! It is a trying, turbulent journey filled with struggles, strains and challenges.

It was not until I started walking with Christ that I experienced people lying on me. It was not until I made Jesus my choice that I learned just how much people will reject, ridicule and minimize you. Moreover, sometimes, it seems easier to turn my back on Jesus and go fit in with everybody else than to stay the course He has set before me. But, the devil is a liar. I am determined to live for Jesus. I am determined to live for God. I am determined not to turn around, but to continue on, full speed ahead.

It is important that we stay the course. Do not dare throw in the towel. In fact, pick up the towel. Wipe the blood, sweat and tears. And keep pushing.

My prayer is that as you read the pages of this book, you will find help to develop, acquire and grow the *faith of a winner*. Just as those patriarchs and matriarchs listed in Scripture, it is possible for you and me to be men and women of faith—and win.

FORMED TO BE A WINNER

A long time ago, an Athenian herald was sent to Sparta to get help when the Persians landed in Greece. It was said that he ran 150 miles in just two days. He would later run another twenty-five miles to announce the victory of the Greeks, at which time he collapsed and died on the spot from exhaustion.

The late Nelson "Mandiba" Mandela campaigned for justice and freedom in his native home of South Africa. As a result, he spent twenty years in jail for his opposition to apartheid.

Michael Jordan, arguably the greatest basketball player of all time, attributes his success to his failures. An unnamed woman, who had an issue of blood for twelve years, spent all her money on a cure, only to be determined incurable. Yet, she decided one day she would touch the hem of one man's garment, believing that she would be made whole from that one touch.

All of these people have one thing in common: they decided not to quit. The Athenian herald is the reason we now have marathons. Mr. Mandela is the reason that South African citizens can live in unity with one another, despite their cultural and skin tone differences. Michael Jordan is the reason why so many of us leap from our tiptoes with our tongues hanging out to shoot the basketball into the hoop. That woman with the issue of blood revealed to us that all it takes is a little tenacity, initiative and faith, and the very thing that has had us perplexed, broken, separated and feeling helpless can be cured.

This book evolved from a sermon I ministered a few years ago and my personal time of devotion as I sought the Lord about faith. I struggle with having faith—sometimes doubt creeps in more often than I care to admit. This book belongs to those people who, like me, are presently, or have lived through, some less-than-stellar times in life. You've seen days of struggle, strain, heartache and pain. You've endured being talked about, ostracized, ridiculed and mocked. If you're like me, you've had to endure a broken heart, your name being scandalized, and the people you loved, trusted and confided in betraying you. But most imperatively, you have had to endure the difficulty of faithlessness.

This book is for you. You represent the hearers to which God wanted to send this message. You, my fellow brothers and sisters, are the ones to whom God has prompted me to deliver this message. Simply put, you were created and formed to be a winner. And there's significant evidence to substantiate my claim.

Genesis 1:26 says, *And God said, "Let us make man in our image, after our likeness..."* Deuteronomy 28:13 says, *And the Lord shall make thee the head, and not the tail; and thou shall be above only, and thou shall not be beneath...* Romans 8:37 reminds us, *Nay, in all these things we are more than conquerors through him that loved us.*

Time and time again in the Word of God, we're assured that we were created to be winners. Yet, for most of us, if we were honest, we have found ourselves in some situations where it appeared, and even felt like, we were losing. We have found ourselves in the midst of battles that we couldn't tell anybody about. For some reading this book, you are so close to the edge that taking too deep a breath could cause you to fall off the cliff. For some, you have tossed and turned all night, unable to get an ounce of sleep because you're worried about life's happenstances.

You may be like millions of other Americans, afraid that the house you live in will soon be taken away through foreclosure, theft or fire. Or perhaps, you are perplexed because of financial, health or marital issues. You may feel overwhelmed by the news that your parents are now divorcing. Your

THE FAITH OF A WINNER

favorite church mother has died. That older sibling is strung out on drugs. Your baby's momma or baby's daddy is now locked up, and you just got laid off. Times when we should have won, we lost. Times when we should have been victorious, we wound up being the victim.

We've all asked the questions: *Why does all this seem to happen to me? What am I lacking? Where did I miss the mark? What ingredient did I lack in this recipe for life? What was the missing link in the chain? What piece am I missing to this puzzled life?*

ANTOINE D. JACKSON

IT IS POSSIBLE FOR YOU

I must admit, there have been times when I have read the Bible and thought to myself, *This could never happen for me*. For instance, when I read the story of David, the shepherd boy turned giant slayer, turned king. On occasion, I found it most difficult to believe that such a transition could happen for me. I know I am not alone because I receive countless emails, texts and social media messages from people who find it hard to believe that God could or would intervene in their lives as He did for the biblical patriarchs and matriarchs.

Think back for a moment. Get a mental picture

of that person in your life who always seems to win. You have likely tried to build a rationale as to why their life is the way it is. Maybe you have wondered what it is that sets this person apart from you. For most of us, we have observed some degree of success in this person. So, what is it that sets those who win in life apart from those who do not? Could it be their faith?

As Christians, we rehearse how powerful our faith is. 1 John 5:4 says, *For whatsoever is born of God overcometh the world: and this is the victory that overcometh the world, even our faith.* Scripture instructs us that we can speak to the mountain, and it will be moved. As children, this particular Scripture reference was drilled into our memory. While many have been taught our faith can move mountains, many others are still out buying mountain climbing gear. Although we cannot see it, touch it, taste it, smell it or hear it, many of us long for more of it. What is faith? How do we get faith? How does faith grow? Scholars, theologians and a large majority of the modern world hold to the definition that faith is having absolute confidence in someone or something.

So what does all this mean to us in our everyday lives? After all, our five physical senses are devoid of the help we so desperately need to understand faith. These are the questions and thoughts we ponder in our minds, leaving us in a continual fight of faith. The good news is that this is quite all right; it is a faith fight we are destined to win.

ANTOINE D. JACKSON

WHAT IS FAITH?

We are in a fight, and it would behoove us to understand for what we are fighting. Hebrews 11:1 best answers the question, "What is faith?" *Now faith is the assurance of what is hoped for, the conviction of what is not seen* (English Standard Version).

Wow, that is a loaded statement! Faith is the assurance, the pledge, guarantee, and certainty of mind that what you do not see, *already is!* Faith is the conviction, the certainty of what is not regarded as already existing. Faith believes that something you cannot see is already yours; you are just waiting for its manifestation.

Mark 9:24 says, *Have faith in God. I assure you: If anyone says to this mountain, 'be lifted up and thrown into the sea,' and does not doubt in his heart, but believes that what he says will happen, it will be done for him.* There's that mountain talk again! Mark 9:25 continues to say, *Therefore, I tell you, all things you pray and ask for believe that you have received them, and you will have them.*

This is one of the most profound verses about faith. Faith believes that you have already received that which you asked for. It is only when you believe in such a way that you will have what you want. Notice that speaking is also a critical component. It has been said that a picture is worth a thousand words. However, those words will undoubtedly become convenient if the picture becomes distorted or its meaning is misunderstood. After all, the most effective way to communicate is through speech. You need to speak the things you want into reality. Talk about what you want as though you already have it!

Let's face it. Faith is an elusive thing. It's very

hard to possess faith in a world where everything seems to go against it. We have a tendency to believe what we see, hear, feel, touch and smell. Our five senses are so strong that they can cause our faith to waver very easily. Our environment speaks doubt, fear and unbelief into us and leaves us unable to possess the things in life we desire. People and circumstances around us destroy our faith and leave us like a ship without a rudder, tossed by the winds of life with little or no sense of direction.

What is it that you really desire? That is the first thing you must focus on. Do not even think about what you *do not* want in life; pay attention to the things you do want. Colossians 3:2 tells us to *set our affections*—this means to set our minds and stay focused habitually. We should ponder them. Think about them. Write them down. Dream about them and speak of them as though you already possess them. Then, you shall have them.

Rid your environment of those who would rather live life in the fray. Stay clear of negative people and places. Because of the day we live in, stay away from negative social media and news outlets. They will only derail your faith.

Jude 1:3 says, *Beloved, while I was making every effort to write you about our common salvation, I was compelled to write to you [urgently] appealing that you fight strenuously for [the defense of] the faith which was once for all handed down to the saints [the faith that is the sum of Christian belief that was given verbally to believers] (Amplified Version).*

The fight is real, but it is a fixed fight. It is a fight you are guaranteed to win as long as you do not give in and throw in the towel.

BY FAITH, NOT BY SIGHT

For we walk by faith, not by sight.
(2 Corinthians 5:7)

Those eight words appear simple enough. But, what does it mean to live by faith? Life has taught me that this can be one of the most challenging tasks to complete. To walk by faith means to live our lives in a manner that is consistent with a confident belief in God's promises. While the task may seem scary to me, the reward of the assignment is great.

Living by faith requires incredible courage and strength. We must be willing to endure being ridiculed, misjudged and, at times, even standing alone. Faith requires us to give up complete control of our lives. One pastor told me, "Antoine, you have to be prepared to look like a fool in the face of your worst critics if you're going to live by faith."

While I cannot assert that I have learned all there is to absorb about faith, I have been able to reach a place of joy and peace when I had to travel life's way, seeing only through the lens of faith. It has, by far, been one of the most rewarding blessings. Though it's a life-altering journey filled with excitement, walking by faith has the tendency to leave me baffled. Walking by faith has allowed me to see God on a level that I could have only previously imagined. Through faith, I experience God as He was intended: in all His fullness and grace. Walking by faith and not by sight requires us to go beyond our place of comfort, into the place that God will reveal as we walk in obedience.

Leaving the Nest

Think about the eaglet whose parent sirs the nest. When an eaglet approaches 10-12 weeks after hatching, the mother eagle will begin to stir, or reconfigure, the nest to cause discomfort and agitation to the newly hatched eaglets. This discomfort is a prompting of sorts—an indicator that it is now time for the eaglets to move beyond the nest and take flight.

Despite their wings lacking strength and their bodies not weighing enough to combat the fierce winds of flying, the mother eagle stirs the nest, gradually urging the eaglets out. At the first sign of the change, the eaglets squeal loudly, but the mother isn't moved by their noise—neither does she stop her work. She continues reconstructing the nest in such a manner as to agitate the eaglets.

Aware that they have little to no ability to stop the mother eagle from making the changes, the eaglets fledge outside of the nest in an effort to find comfort. Like humans, the eaglets encounter the physiological response of "fight or flight" in response to perceived harm or a threat.

Their initial fledging is usually to a nearby branch, but they usually don't leave the tree.

Perhaps they hope that she will soon discontinue her stirring. The mother eagle, still not satisfied, doesn't stop stirring. In fact, she rattles nearby branches to disturb the eaglets and shoo them into flying. After a few days of fledging from the nest to a branch, and vice versa, the eaglets finally take off in short flight. They soon return to the nest, repeating this routine for approximately two months. Finally, there comes a day when the eaglets take off from the nest to explore parts unknown, returning to the nest approximately a year later.

The mother eagle's role in her eaglets' lives has now come to an end. She has done her duty to incubate, feed, nurture and force out her eaglets to be what they were always created to be—birds that fly. The process to get the eaglet out of the nest seems inhumane and may be frowned upon if a human parent created such agitation for their child. However, this is the way of life, the path that many will take in order to impact the world greatly.

Are you ready to soar beyond the nest and trees of your hatching? Your faith will grow stronger as you embrace the truth of being a winner. If you are looking for someone to tell you that it's time to shine, I already did that in *100-Watt Life: No Longer Hidden. Positioned to Shine and Flip the Switch*, two of my other books. Now is the time to increase your faith as you shine.

Leaving the nest is a monumental moment in our lives. It is the moment that we go fledging into the world to find our place and rhythm. Just as the eaglet, we squeal at the stirring that takes place. Our squeals translate into complaints, broken focus and wavering in our faith. Nevertheless, the stirring continues—not to kill us—but to push us into being the people we were created to be. The mother eagle knew that her eaglets were born to fly. So when the opportunity arose, it was her responsibility to push them to become who she already knew they were destined to be.

In like fashion, God knew us before we knew ourselves. When the opportunity arose, it became His responsibility to push us into who He already knew we were—winners. In fact, He tells us in

Jeremiah 1:5, *Before I formed thee in the belly I knew thee.*

Leaving the nest is an opportunity for us to get to know ourselves. It's an opportunity for us to explore our environment and to make an impact in the earth. As long as the eaglet was in the nest, he never knew the strength of his wings. He never tapped into his innate ability to soar. He never got to experience the beauty of the landscape. The push, the stirring, helped him discover himself.

When we live by faith, we discover our real identity. We learn who we were always meant to be, according to the Father. Although scary and sometimes intimidating, moving through life by faith is how we are supposed to live.

LIVING WITH EXPECTATION

Are the best days of our lives behind us or in front of us? Our outlook on life, our answer to that question, can change over time. When we were teenagers, we couldn't wait to grow up. However, when we were introduced to adulthood and adopted the responsibilities of work, bills and a family, we found ourselves wishing we could go back to being a child.

No matter our age, when we walk with God, we should live in expectation of what's to come. This is not to denounce what He has done, or to be unappreciative of what God is currently doing. It is simply an acknowledgement that you can depend on

God, the one who holds tomorrow, to bring about the best for you. As a result, our daily declaration should be, "The best is yet to come!"

Unfortunately, we live in a world where we are repeatedly taught to live without expectation. Motivational speakers, Alcoholics Anonymous group leaders, and psychologists alike have taught us, through maladaptive quotes that urge us to resist the innate desire, to expect. While it is in our nature to expect, we are taught to lower our expectations, or get rid of them altogether.

When I visited a residential home for youth who struggled with addiction, I was surprised to see a poster in the general seating area that read: "The secret of happiness is low expectations." Another read: "Expectations are premeditated resentments." These quotes lead us to believe that to live life in expectancy is to live in preparation for a negative experience. These quotes lead us to believe that to live a life of expectation is, in some way, a setup for failure or disappointment. Perhaps some teach us to not expect based upon their limited experiences and the persons in whom their expectations resided in the past. Perhaps their learnings about expectation came through a negative experience with someone or something.

Maybe they expected their father or mother to love and care for them, but they failed them and abandoned them. Perhaps it was their spouse who, instead of remaining committed to the marriage vows, stepped outside the marriage. Maybe it was an experience with an employer who handed them a pink slip or layoff notice. Maybe it was a vehicle they purchased, which seemed to be in mint condition, but before they could get past the first block, it shut down. For some, it was the knowledge of knowing that they themselves could not live up to their own expectations.

Whatever the case, their expectations have been diminished or doused altogether. So now, their ability to see life through the lens of expectation is difficult. Now, they live in a state of constant apprehension and caution, instead of expectation and faith.

This is counterintuitive to our Bible teaching. Again, remember, For we walk by faith, not by sight. Living by faith means you trust that God is who He says He is and that we are a part of His plan. Because of this, I expect. Expectations are rooted in the presumption that God will work things out for our good.

Nevertheless, when we are faced with unfulfilled expectations, we are forced to face disappointment. We, in turn, become despondent to the idea that anything good will happen for us. This is not always an intentional thing, but it happens. In fact, psychologists have concluded that when we encounter numerous negative situations or outcomes, we develop an appetite or a kind of a reverse-expectation for more negativity, therefore causing us to live in a state of apprehension.

On the contrary, Charles Franklin Kettering, an American inventor, engineer, businessman, and the holder of 186 patents, lets us in on a secret. He's responsible for founding what we know today as AC/Delco, and he served as former head of research at General Motors from 1920 to 1947. His secret, though complex, is very simple: "High achievement always takes place in the framework of high expectation."

You will never achieve greatness with a low expectation.

You will never see higher heights and deeper depths with small expectations.

You will never accomplish anything without having a high degree of expectation.

Whether spiritual or natural, expectation is the fuel that moves us from one level to the next. Expectation is the water that quenches our thirst as we face dry places. It is expectation that will cause me to get up in the morning at 5 a.m. and head to the gym before day breaks because I expect to see something different when I look in the mirror.

The writer of Psalm 27:13 knew a thing or two about the power of expectation. There, he says, *I had fainted, unless I had believed (expected) to see the goodness of the Lord in the land of the living.* Your expectation will give life to your fragile bones, joy to your depressed heart, and stability to your wavering mind. Before you imply that I'm giving too much credit to expectation, let's consider the power of expectation in Scripture. Acts 12 details the arrest and subsequent release of Peter from jail. It is in that story that we learn that Peter was delivered by God, from all expectation of the people. Here, my brothers and sisters, we can see one instance where God intervened because of the expectations of the people. Not only here, but throughout Scripture, we see this time and time again—God delivering people from the expectation of others. In these passages, we see just how powerful expectation is.

But it is in our principal text that it is revealed to us the reasons why we sometimes find it difficult to live a life of expectancy. The Apostle Paul, in his letter to the church at Rome, addresses this issue in Romans 8:1-2: *There is therefore now no condemnation to them which are in Christ Jesus, who walk not after the flesh, but after the Spirit. For the law of the Spirit of life in Christ Jesus hath made me free from the law of sin and death.* Paul reveals to us that, in order to live a life of expectancy, we have to understand that the past is over!

Paul urges us that there is, in this moment, no disapproval of us who we are in Christ Jesus. In fact, he goes on to say the, *Law of the Spirit of Life in Christ: had made us free.* That tells me that my freedom has nothing to do with you or me. As a matter of fact, it isn't even a fleshly thing; it's all spiritual. Therefore, I'm no longer bound under guilt and shame. No longer do I have to live with my head down or my hands cuffed by the guilt of my past. I can live free in Christ Jesus. No longer should I be looking at the future through the lens of my past, causing me to view the future with apprehension, instead of expectation. Let it go!

Our inability to accept this news keeps us hostage, keeps us living a life of apprehension and not expectation. Make no mistake about it. We are all challenged with accepting that our past has been forgiven; overcoming this challenge is not easy. The main reason this is so difficult is because we are ruled by guilt and held captive psychologically by our past. Everywhere we turn, there is something or someone to remind us of our past. It may be your ex-spouse, the child born out of wedlock, your criminal record, your resume or the pictures. But, none of that matters here!

That chapter is over. The book is done. Write new pages. Yes, we will be constantly reminded of our past. But, we must pull from Paul's writing in Philippians 3:13: *Brethren, I count not myself to have apprehended: but this one thing I do, forgetting those things which are behind, and reaching forth unto those things which are before...* Living a life of expectation requires forgetting the past.

Our principal text reveals to us another reason why we find it difficult to live a life of expectancy. Another challenge we so often encounter is in who or what we hang our expectations upon. Surely, if you hang your expectations upon me, I may very well disappoint you. It's impossible for me not to fail in my flesh. It is impossible for me not to do something to offend you or cause you to feel disheartened. Yet many of us continue to put our hopes and expectations in people.

Knowing this, the writer in Psalm 20:7 warns us: *Some trust in chariots, and some in horses: but we will remember the name of the Lord our God.* Even more, the writer in Psalm 62:5 encourages himself when he says, *My soul, wait thou only upon God; for my expectation is from him.* In Psalm 118:8, possibly having had a negative experience, the writer lets us know, *It is better to trust in the Lord than to put confidence in man.* Don't hang your expectations on the shakiness of fickle, inconsistent men and women. Our hope and trust must be in God.

Therefore, Paul lets us know that we are free from the past because we are now in Christ Jesus. In his writing, Paul asserts to us the power of the gospel. Primarily, he reveals to us that the gospel promises the future, in spite of the past. God is not hindered by what you did yesterday when you have repented today. As a matter of fact, when God called you, He was fully aware of your past, present and future. Yet, He still called you.

Therefore, Paul lets us in on this when he clarifies that we are made free from sin through Jesus. He tells us in Romans 8:3-4, *For what the law could not do, in that it was weak through the flesh, God sending his own Son in the likeness of sinful flesh, and for sin, condemned sin in the flesh: That the righteousness of the law might be fulfilled in us, who walk not after the flesh, but after the Spirit.* So, since I'm free from sin, I now walk in a new direction. No longer do I walk in the darkness of yesterday, but I walk in the light of today. I'm no longer tied to the hiccups of my past, but my thirst has been quenched by the living waters of Christ.

As such, Paul tells us that we have to change the way we think. He says in Romans 8:5-6, *For they that are after the flesh do mind the things of the flesh; but they that are after the Spirit the things of the Spirit. For to be carnally minded is death; but to be spiritually minded is life and peace.* We must release our old ways of thinking. We must strive to live with our spirit and conscience clean and clear. In his letter to the church at Corinth, Paul said in 2 Corinthians 4:1-2, *Therefore, since we have this ministry, just as we received mercy, we do not get discouraged nor lose our motivation. But we have renounced the disgraceful things hidden because of shame; not walking in trickery or adulterating the word of God, but by stating the truth [openly and plainly], we commend ourselves to everyone's conscience in the sight of God* (Amplified Bible).

This, my brothers and sisters, must be the action of all those who will live a life of expectancy. Paul urges us that since God has raised Jesus from the dead, He shall likewise raise us up. When we find ourselves entombed by trouble, we don't have to fear because God will get us up. When we are faced with insurmountable odds—folk lying on you, financial distress, sickness, stress or strain—we can trust that God will see us through.

Paul tells us that he reckons. This simply means based on everything I have seen God do before, I have come to the calculated conclusion that things will get better. Yes, we are living in perilous times, and the Bible speaks of things getting worse. However, God promised me that I would not have to endure the perils alone. When my burdens get too heavy, I can go to God in prayer. When things are seemingly up above my head and out of my reach, I can look to the hills from whence cometh my help. All of my help comes from the Lord. For the Lord is my light and my salvation. Whom shall I fear? The Lord is the strength of my life. Of whom shall I be afraid? Therefore, I expect it to happen!

That new job. I expect it to happen!

Peace in my mind. I expect it to happen!

Joy instead of pain. I expect it to happen!

Graduating high school. I expect it to happen!

Finishing my degrees. I expect it to happen!

I am no longer tied to the past. In fact, my pastor often reminds me the past is a canceled check, tomorrow is a promissory note, but today is cash in hand. I'm standing on the promise that it will happen. Just as he spoke to the Prophet Jeremiah to tell the people in exile, in Jeremiah 29:11, he speaks to us today: *"For I know the thoughts that I think toward you,' saith the Lord, 'thoughts of peace, and not of evil, to give you an expected end."*

So no matter how dark it gets, how bad it turns, I expect God to see me through. I join with Paul in Romans 8:28 when he said, *And we know that all things work together for good to them that love God, to them who are the called according to his purpose.*

ANTOINE D. JACKSON

THE PRINCIPLES

The Christian life is a life of faith. We are known by two things: our love for one another and our faith. We are the seed of Abraham.

There is one attribute that characterizes Abraham's descendants—faith. I found five fundamental principles of faith.

God is the Initiator of Faith

Faith is our response to what God initiates on our behalf. God initiates; we respond. The great heroes of faith, such as Noah, Moses and Joshua, responded to God's particular call upon their lives. Some believe and teach that their faith causes things to happen. When we believe in something God has not initiated and try to get God to respond to our so-called faith by giving us what we want, we are not in the realm of faith, but manipulation.

Jesus demonstrated the life of faith on earth. *Then answered Jesus and said unto them, Verily, verily, I say unto you, The Son can do nothing of himself, but what he seeth the Father do: for what things soever he doeth, these also doeth the Son likewise* (John 5:19). Everything Jesus did was in response to that which His Father initiated. He chose the disciples because His Father told Him to. He turned the water into wine because the Father told Him to. He went through Samaria because the Father told Him to. He never did anything on His own initiative. This is the model for the life of faith. The life of faith consists of learning more of His truth and His ways concerning our lives and responding to that.

Faith Must Have a Focus

People try to live by faith in faith. But faith must

have an object in which to trust, a place in which to put confidence. Faith enables me to hold on to my object. In this way, faith takes us out of ourselves. Believing is not the issue with faith. What you believe, is. Is the object of your faith worthy of your trust? Will it fulfill your expectations? The strength of our faith is determined by the strength of the object. What happens when the object of your faith fails you? You are reluctant to trust that object again.

Faith in God only fails when people have a faulty expectation of Him. Faith seems to fail when people want Him to do *their* thing, not *His*. True faith means believing what God has said, not what we want Him to do. The certainty of faith comes from the fact that God cannot lie. Numbers 23:19 says, *God is not a man that he should lie; neither the son of man, that he should repent: hath he said, and shall he not do it? Or hath he spoken, and shall he not make it good?*

Christ is the Prime Focus of Our Faith

What is the focus of your faith? To what did God direct Abraham's faith? He promised in Genesis 12:3, *In you, all the families of the earth shall be blessed.* When God called Abraham, He began His program for worldwide redemption. All the families of the world would be blessed, but how? Abraham and Sarah were promised seed. It is toward that seed that God directed Abraham's faith. What did the promise of seed mean?

God gave promises to Abraham regarding his natural seed. i.e. the people and the land of Israel. Isaac was only the beginning of this seed. Abraham was also promised spiritual seed. But Christ is the Seed to which God referred. He is the Seed that was promised from the beginning in Eden (Genesis 3:15). He is the Seed par excellence. Abraham failed many times. Abraham was not righteous because of his obedience, but because He believed in Christ, the Seed. To have the kind of faith Abraham had is to become his seed.

The prime object of our faith is Christ. In the

entire Old Testament, which takes up about 80% of the Bible, faith is mentioned only 15 times. The reason is that the prime object of our faith, Jesus Christ, had not yet come to earth. Faith had not yet been revealed.

Grace is the Partner to Faith

Grace and faith go hand in hand. They are partners, associates. Faith is the counterpart, the complement to grace. It is by grace *through* faith. Grace is God's side; faith is our side. Grace is what He has done. Faith is not what we have to do, but how we receive what He has done. These two belong together and cannot be separated. If it is of grace, then it is by faith.

Thanksgiving is the Language of Faith

God gave Abraham another promise concerning land. In response to that promise, he built an altar and worshiped the Lord, thanking Him for His promise, as if he had already received it. Yet, the Canaanites were still in the land.

We, too, offer sacrifices. Hebrews 13:15 says, *Therefore by Him let us continually offer the sacrifice of praise to God, that is, the fruit of our lips, giving thanks to His name.* We are exhorted in 1 Thessalonians 5:18: *In everything, give thanks.* Don't just thank Him for what He has done, but for what He is going to do. Thank Him for making us sufficient for all things.

Complaining is the language of unbelief. Thanksgiving is the language of faith. Also, in our prayers, pleading is the language of unbelief. We offer supplications with thanksgivings according to Philippians 4:6. According to Colossians 4:2, *We continue earnestly in prayer, being vigilant in it with thanksgiving.*

A FINAL WORD ON FAITH

In a society that teaches us to "Live how you want to and God will be okay with it," it's hard to accept as true that there is something I can do that would displease God. The world teaches us that we are free from displeasing God and that our actions, no matter how drastic or against His Word, will never separate us from God. Many have taken on the mindset that grace is a free pass to live how we want. On the contrary, grace has standards. Isaiah 59:2 teaches us *your wickedness has separated you from your God, and your sins have hidden His face from you so that He does not hear.* Not only will our sins separate us from Him, but also our lack of faith displeases or offends Him. This is difficult to digest. However, it's fact.

Did not Jesus die for my sins? Did not He take away the curse of the law? Did not He rid my soul of the condemnation that separated me from God? The answer to all those questions is yes. However, it is our faith in the finished work of Christ that makes us heirs. After all, God through His son Jesus, has saved us from our sins, and through our confession, according to Romans 10:9-10, we are afforded the opportunity to live in eternity with Him. *But without faith it is impossible to please him: for he that cometh to God must believe that he is, and that he is a rewarder of them that diligently seek him* (Hebrews 11:6). It is said that without this faith it is impossible to please God. But what is "this faith" that the writer speaks of? It is a faith that helps us to walk with God. It is an active faith. Our faith must believe that God is. He is what He is, as revealed in the scriptures. God exists in three persons, Father, Son and Holy Ghost, and is a being of immeasurable Excellency. Our faith must witness to and accept the concrete belief that God exists. Devoid of this faith, we cannot come to God unless we believe that He is, and that He is a rewarder of those that diligently seek Him. This is the *faith of a winner!*

ABOUT THE AUTHOR

Antoine D. Jackson is a young, influential minister, author, entrepreneur and mentor. He is a preacher and teacher that God has anointed to support, and encourage believers and nonbelievers alike. His desire is to exhort and evangelize others to a relationship with Jesus Christ. Antoine serves on the ministerial staff at Greater Mitchell Temple Church of God in Christ in Detroit, Michigan under the spiritual tutelage of Bishop John Henry Sheard.

Antoine is a native of Detroit, Michigan where he resides with his beautiful daughter. Antoine is a nonprofit professional leader for a major global organization that serves intellectually disabled youth and adults. He enjoys spending time with his daughter, graphic design, music, time with family and friends, writing and mentoring.

ANTOINE D. JACKSON

#FAITHOFAWINNER

Keep the Conversation Going!

Visit Antoine via his social media profiles.

BLOG

Antoinejacskon.blogspot.com

FACEBOOK

Facebook.com/authorantoinejackson

TWITTER & PERISCOPE

@ElderADJackson

YOUTUBE

YouTube.com/MinisterADJackson

ANTOINE D. JACKSON

THE PRAYER OF SALVATION

Salvation through Jesus Christ is available to whosoever will. I thank God for you taking the time to read this book. I pray that something within this work has provided you with strength, vigor and encouragement to continue in this race to follow Christ. All the same, I understand that you may be reading this book and have not accepted the Lord Jesus Christ as your personal savior and I want to present to you the opportunity to do so right now. Pray this prayer:

Lord Jesus, come into my heart. Lord I repent and turn from all of my sins and all of my unrighteous behavior. Lord, I ask that you create in me a clean heart and renew a right spirit within me. Lord, I confess with my mouth the Lord Jesus Christ and I believe in my heart that you have raised Jesus from the dead. Lord, I believe that you will return to this earth to gather those who have confessed you that we may live in eternity with you in heaven. Lord, I am sorry for my actions, words, thoughts, and emotions that have been contrary to your will. Lord, save me right now, in Jesus' name! Amen!

If you prayed that prayer to God with sincerity and in faith, the bible says that you are now saved, and born again. Set free from the bondage of sin! I encourage you to find a bible-teaching church congregation and join it if you have not already done so. Even if you already know the Lord as your savior, and this prayer has served as a reminder of your commitment to God and His love towards you, I encourage you to remain faithful in the call that God has placed on your life.

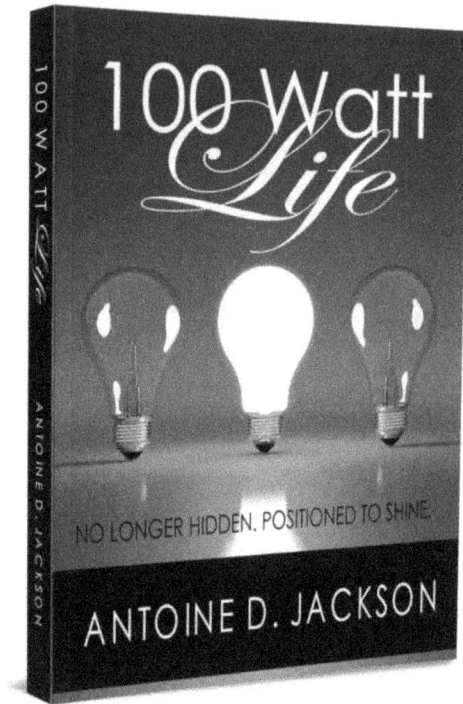

"Flip the switch. Change the bulb. What ever you do, make up your mind to shine."
- Antoine Jackson, 100-Watt Life, 2013

Available at bookstores everywhere, or at **AntoineJackson.org**

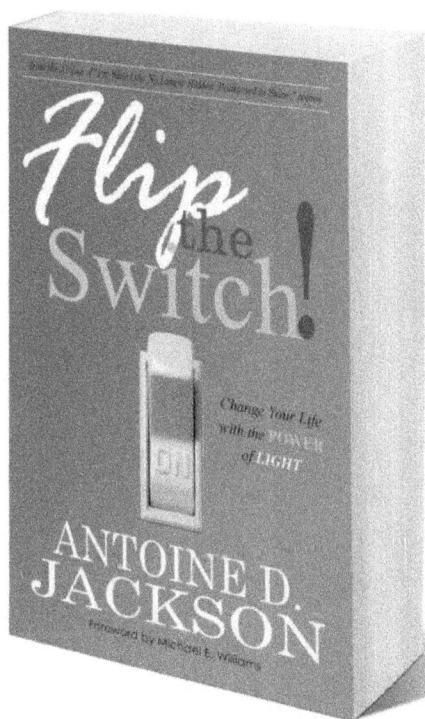

"And God said, Let there be light: and there was light." What are you waiting on? - Antoine Jackson, Flip The Switch, 2014

Available at bookstores everywhere, or at **AntoineJackson.org**

ANTOINE D. JACKSON

Reflections on the *faith of a winner*!

_____

_____

_____

_____

_____

_____

_____

_____

_____

_____

_____

_____

_____

_____

_____

_____

_____

_____

_____

_____

_____

_____

_____

_____

_____

_____

_____

_____

_____

_____

_____

_____

Reflections on the *faith of a winner*!

_____
_____
_____
_____
_____
_____
_____
_____
_____
_____
_____
_____
_____
_____
_____
_____
_____
_____
_____
_____
_____
_____
_____
_____
_____
_____

Reflections on the *faith of a winner*!

_____
_____
_____
_____
_____
_____
_____
_____
_____
_____
_____
_____
_____
_____
_____
_____
_____
_____
_____
_____
_____
_____
_____
_____
_____
_____
_____
_____
_____

Reflections on the *faith of a winner*!

_____
_____
_____
_____
_____
_____
_____
_____
_____
_____
_____
_____
_____
_____
_____
_____
_____
_____
_____
_____
_____
_____
_____
_____
_____
_____
_____
_____

Reflections on the *faith of a winner*!

_____

_____

_____

_____

_____

_____

_____

_____

_____

_____

_____

_____

_____

_____

_____

_____

_____

_____

_____

_____

_____

_____

_____

_____

_____

_____

_____

_____

_____

_____

Reflections on the *faith of a winner*!

_____

_____

_____

_____

_____

_____

_____

_____

_____

_____

_____

_____

_____

_____

_____

_____

_____

_____

_____

_____

_____

_____

_____

_____

_____

_____

_____

_____

_____

_____

_____

_____

_____

____Reflections on the *faith of a winner*!

_____

_____

_____

_____

_____

_____

_____

_____

_____

_____

_____

_____

_____

_____

_____

_____

_____

_____

_____

_____

_____

_____

_____

_____

_____

_____

_____

_____

_____

Reflections on the *faith of a winner*!

_____
_____
_____
_____
_____
_____
_____
_____
_____
_____
_____
_____
_____
_____
_____
_____
_____
_____
_____
_____
_____
_____
_____
_____
_____
_____
_____
_____
_____

Reflections on the *faith of a winner*!

_____

_____

_____

_____

_____

_____

_____

_____

_____

_____

_____

_____

_____

_____

_____

_____

_____

_____

_____

_____

_____

_____

_____

_____

_____

_____

_____

_____

_____

_____

Reflections on the *faith of a winner*!

THE FAITH OF A WINNER

ANTOINE D. JACKSON

www.ingramcontent.com/pod-product-compliance
Lightning Source LLC
Chambersburg PA
CBHW031342040426
42443CB00006B/438